Study Guide

for

Teach Me, Lord, to Dance
An Interview with Jesus

Karen Pettingell, Ph.D.

Frankie Dove Publishing
Federal Way, Washington

Study Guide
for
Teach Me, Lord, to Dance: An Interview with Jesus
Copyright © 2007 by Frankie Dove Publishing.

All rights reserved,
including the right of reproduction
in whole or in part in any form.

Cover design by Cathi Stevenson.

Scripture taken from the HOLY BIBLE,
NEW INTERNATIONAL VERSION®
Copyright © 1973, 1978, 1984 International Bible Society.
Used by permission of Zondervan. All rights reserved.

Scripture quotations marked (NLT) are taken from the Holy Bible,
New Living Translation, copyright © 1996.
Used by permission of Tyndale House Publishers, Inc.,
Wheaton, Illinois 60189. All rights reserved.

Printed in the United States of America.
ISBN: 978-0-9786487-1-8

Library of Congress Control Number: 2007904028

For information about special discounts for bulk purchases,
please contact Frankie Dove Publishing at

Frankie Dove Publishing
P.O. Box 3875
Federal Way, Washington 98063
www.frankiedove.com

Study Guide

for

Teach Me, Lord, to Dance
An Interview with Jesus

Talking Points

Forward 7

1 You were a radical, weren't you? 9

2 Why did you heal? 13

3 What did you teach? 15

4 Your mother was a virgin? 19

5 Did you ever get angry? 23

6 Tell me about your disciples. 27

7 How did you die? 31

8 You didn't stay dead, did you? 35

9 Why did you go through all this? 39

10 What is hell like? 43

11 What is heaven like? 47

12 When are you coming back? 49

13 Why is prayer important? 53

14 Why is worship important? 57

15 You want me to smell good? 61

16 You want me to wear the emperor's clothes? 67

17 Your Majesty! 71

Forward

Our prayer is that as you go through this study guide you'll experience immense delight in reading and studying the Bible. Each chapter has two parts. The Discussion section is to get a better understanding of various teachings in the Scriptures related to the chapter. This section is also written to be talked about in groups if desired.

The Application section of each chapter is written to encourage each of you to personalize what is being studied. If others may accidentally see your answers, feel free to change names and settings in some of your answers. The goal is to bring all concerns to the Lord. Never is the study to be a time for gossip or accidental hurt.

Psalm 1:1-2 states our goals best. "Blessed is the man who does not walk in the counsel of the wicked or stand in the way of sinners or sit in the seat of mockers. But his delight is in the law of the LORD, and on his law he meditates day and night." (NIV) We desire that each person reading *Teach Me, Lord, to Dance* and this study guide meditate on the Bible (God's law) day and night.

David sang praises in Psalm 9:1-2, "I will praise you, O LORD, with all my heart; I will tell of all your wonders. I will be glad and rejoice in you; I will sing praise to your name, O Most High." (NIV) May each of you burst with awe and praise of the Lord as you study Him in these pages.

Yours in Christ,

Karen Pettingell, PhD.

You were a radical, weren't you?

Read chapter 1.
Read the Scriptures on p. 167 for chapter 1.

Discussion

1. Radical

    a. Do you think Jesus was a radical? Why?

    b. Do you think He would be a radical today? Why?

2. What would be the equivalent of turning over the money changers' tables today?

3. Using the definition of "meek" on page 21, discuss the Beatitude in Matthew 5:5.

4. Characteristics Jesus didn't like: hypocrites, self-righteous, self-important, intolerant religious people, those who became rich at the expense of others, and self-impressed professionals.

   a. Jesus associated with these people, but what was His attitude toward them?

   b. What standards did Jesus set for us to interact with these individuals?

Application

   c. Which of these characteristics that Jesus doesn't like do you have all the time or from time-to-time?

d. How should I handle traits Jesus doesn't like in me?

5. How did Jesus describe "meek?" See page 21 and Matthew 5:1-11 especially verse 5.

   a. Who did Jesus serve?

   b. How did Jesus talk about His "power under control?"

   c. How am I to have "power under control?"

   d. Who am I to serve?

Why did you heal?

Read chapter 2.
Read the Scriptures on p. 168 for chapter 2.

Discussion

1. Have you experienced a healing or know of one? If so describe it.

2. How do you think you would have reacted to Jesus' healing?

3. John 11:1-44 talks of Lazarus' being raised from the dead. What did Jesus mean when He said, "And, the Father received the greater glory because of it," (John 11:4 and 40)?

Application

a. If I were Martha and my brother was dead and buried and then Jesus brought Him back to life, I would react...[finish]

b. My reaction would/would-not [circle one] bring God glory, praise and honor because...[finish]

4. Jesus did not heal or perform miracles for the "wow" factor.

    a. What does this mean?

    b. What do I do to get the "wow" reaction from others?

    c. As a Christian all I do should follow Christ's example. How should I react to praise and criticism in daily life to avoid the "wow" factor motivating my actions?

What did you teach?

Read chapter 3.
Read the Scriptures on p. 168 for chapter 3.

Discussion

1. What does the first and great commandment in Matthew 22:37-38 mean literally (i.e. put these verses in your own words)? What does it mean to a believer?

2. What does the second commandment in Matthew 22:39 mean literally? What does it mean to a believer?

3. Relate these two commandments to the commandments given in Deuteronomy 5:6-21.

   a. Compare Matthew 22:37-38 and Deuteronomy 5:6-15.

   b. Compare Matthew 22:39 and Deuteronomy 5:16-21.

Application

4. On page 31 (see also Mark 2:17) Jesus' response is, "He sent me to people who live broken lives, to those who are blind and deaf, who are tired and bound with chains of guilt and misery."

   a. I can relate to this statement because I've...[finish]

   b. Jesus' teaching tells me to handle my guilt and shame by...[finish]

5. I want to love God with all of my heart, all of my soul, and all of my strength. To do this I must...[finish]

6. I am to love my neighbor as I love myself.

    a. It is so hard to love someone enough to listen closely and intently to them. Specifically I can listen to _____ and be a good neighbor to him/her by (describe how you will listen and care for them)...

    b. I must love me.

        i. I don't love me when I....[finish]

        ii. I need to change this by... [finish]

Your mother was a virgin?

Read chapter 4.
Read the Scriptures on p. 169 for chapter 4.

Discussion

1. Imagine you are a Rabbi in the temple and Jesus is talking in Luke 2:41–52.

    a. How would you as a learned adult react to a twelve year old teaching you?

    b. How do you think Jesus got so wise and had so much knowledge by twelve years old?

2. How do you imagine Jesus as a child?

3. What do you think Jesus meant in His response to the question He posed, "Who are my mother and my brothers?" (Mark 3:34-35)

Application

4. On p. 49 Jesus replies in the interview, "Believe me, I will forgive all the hurts you have caused to other people, all the wrong thoughts that have ever gone through your mind, if you let me. I am not delusional. I don't pat you on the back and say it's okay, when its not." Read I Peter 2:1-3.

   a. I have (Confess and acknowledge something from the list above or Peter's list. Be specific and brutally honest.)...[finish]

   b. I must pray for Jesus to forgive me. Write prayer here.

5. The second to the last paragraph in this chapter talks of our spiritual eyes and understanding spiritual things after we confess our sins to Jesus and acknowledge Him as God and Savior. In I Peter 2:1-3 we are told to crave pure spiritual milk (e.g. by reading the Bible).

   a. I want to see others, especially (name someone here or code their name if others might see this page) _____, with spiritual eyes as Jesus sees them because...[finish]

   b. I want to study the Bible and be around other believers so I can understand (name some characteristic of God that you want to learn more about e.g. His love that forgives my sins or e.g. God as Abba Father) because...[finish]

Did you ever get angry?

Read chapter 5.
Read the Scriptures on p. 170 for chapter 5.

Discussion

1. Do you think Jesus laughed? Is there anything in your daily walk with Him that makes Him smile or laugh?

2. Read the passage in chapter 5 pages 55-56 that talks about Jesus weeping.

    a. What do you think makes Him weep in current world events involving Israel and the United States?

    b. What makes Him weep in a believer's life?

Application

3. On page 56 Jesus says, "My heart went out to them. They were like sheep without a shepherd. I wanted to become their Shepherd, to share God's love with them."

   a. Read Matthew 18:10-14. What do you learn about Jesus in this passage?

   b. Because Jesus deeply desired to save lost people (sinners), I must follow His example and (be specific)…[finish]

   c. Finish the following prayer asking God to guide you. Lord, I love You and want to follow Your example. Help me…

4. On page 57 Jesus told Peter, "...you're thinking like everyone else, you're not thinking like God."

    a. Read Mark 8:31-37.

        i. What was the context of this statement?

        ii. What do you think Jesus meant by verse 33?

    b. Verses 34-37 tell me that I must...[finish]

    c. Write a prayer about what you've learned in verses 34-37.

Tell me about your disciples.

Read chapter 6.
Read the Scriptures on p. 171 for chapter 6.

Discussion

1. Read Luke 7:36–50. People and their animals walked along the paths Jesus walked. Imagine how dirty sandaled feet became.

    a. What do you think the woman's hair was like after cleaning Jesus' feet?

    b. Describe the depth of emotions of the following individuals and give reasons for your answer.

        i. The woman

        ii. Simon

iii. Jesus

2. What do you think Jesus meant when He said, "Your faith has saved you, go in peace" in verse 50?

3. The twelve disciples were from various jobs and walks in life. These were His inner circle. What does Jesus' example mean for the leadership in our churches?

Application

4. Read Luke 14:25-33. Jesus tells us we must love Him more than our own father, mother, children, brothers and sisters.

    a. Why?

TELL ME ABOUT YOUR DISCIPLES. 29

b. This means I am to...[finish]

c. I show Jesus I love Him more than any relative or friend by...[finish]

d. A benefit my relatives and friends receive of my loving Jesus most is...[finish]

e. Read verses 28–32. I must count the costs of serving Jesus first and serving Him boldly because...[finish]

f. I want to finish each task the Lord asks me to do.

   i. One task He now is asking me to do is...[finish]

   ii. The cost for me to do this is...[finish]

   iii. I can/cannot [circle one] think of anything more important than doing the Lord's work.

   iv. My plan to accomplish this task is (don't forget prayer)...[finish]

How did you die?

Read chapter 7.
Read the Scriptures on p. 172 for chapter 7.

Discussion

1. Read John 19:28-37 (especially verse 34), Isaiah 53:5 and I Peter 2:23-25.

    a. Specifically state how Christ's blood was shed.

    b. Why was it necessary for Christ's blood to be shed?

    c. What do you think "You have been healed by His wounds" (I Peter 2:24 New Living Translation) means?

2. Many events in the Bible are shadows of future major events. These shadows give us insights to the larger events. Passover is a shadow of Christ's death and shed blood. Read Exodus 11, Exodus 12:1-13, Exodus 12:21-23, Exodus 12:29-30 (the skipped passages describe the Feast of Unleaven Bread/Passover and are very interesting to read), Romans 3:22-25, Ephesians 1:7-8, and I Peter 1:18-20.

   a. Describe the lambs that were sacrificed in the Exodus passages.

   b. Sin is an undesirable blemish in our lives. Describe Christ our Passover lamb regarding sin (blemishes).

   c. How does the lamb's blood parallel Christ's blood?

Application

3. The lamb lived with the family from the tenth of the month to the fourteenth. During this time the lamb became a cherished, beloved pet.

    a. How does this relate to Christ's relationship to the Father?

    b. How do you think the Father felt when He saw Christ on the cross?

    c. Personally relate how the Passover gives you an insight to Christ dying on the cross.

    d. Write a prayer to the Father thanking Him for His precious Lamb (Christ).

e. If you do not know Jesus as your personal Savior and have not asked Him to forgive your sins then please read chapter 18 on page 161.

4. Jesus prayed often and long to the Father.

   a. Personally...

      i. Do you have a friend you can talk to like Jesus did the Father?

      ii. What is it like to talk to this friend?

      iii. What qualities in your friend make it easy to talk to them?

   b. Now use the above answers and finish, "I deeply desire to talk and pray to the Lord because He is...

   c. Write a prayer thanking the Lord for these qualities you just mentioned.

You didn't stay dead, did you?

Read chapter 8.
Read the Scriptures on p. 173 for chapter 8.

Discussion

1. Read John 2:19-22, I Corinthians 3:16-17 and I Corinthians 6:19–20.

    a. What do these Scriptures have to say about "temple?"

    b. As the temple of God each believer has responsibilities (I Corinthians 6:19-20). What are they?

2. Read Matthew 27:57-66, Mark 15:42-47, Luke 23:50-56, and John 19:38-42.

   a. How were Jesus' burial arrangements affected by the Sabbath?

   b. What precautions did the Romans make and why?

3. Why was Jesus' resurrection crucial?

4. Read John 3:16, Romans 6:5-10, Galatians 2:20 and Philippians 3:7-11.

   a. John 3:16 tells us that the death of our body is not the end. It actually is the beginning of...[finish]

b. Romans 6:5-10.

   i. Write Romans 6:5-10 in your own words.

   ii. How does this relate to the last response to the interviewer's question in this chapter?

c. Galatians 2:20.

   i. Write Paul's words in your own words.

Application

    ii.   Paul's witness in this verse tells me that I should...[finish]

  d.   Read Philippians 3:7-11. Like Paul says in this passage, I want to...[finish]

Why did you go through all this?

Read chapter 9.
Read the Scriptures on p. 173 for chapter 9.

Discussion

1. Who do you say God is?

2. Who is God the Father?

3. Who is God the Son?

4. Who is God the Holy Spirit?

5. Read John 10:22-30.

   a. What does Christ say about unbelievers?

Application

   b. Rewrite Christ's words from a believer's point of view, e.g. I hear Christ's voice and know His Word (the Bible).

   c. Write a praise filled prayer of thanksgiving based on your answer to the previous question.

6. Read John 3:17-21.

   a. Finish this statement. I am reassured by John 3:17 because...

b. John 3:18 compares those who are condemned with those who are not. Rewrite verse 18 in your own words.

c. John 3:19-21 compares light and darkness.

   i. Define those who walk in light and those who walk in darkness in your own words.

   ii. I desire to walk in light/darkness [circle one] because... [finish]

What is hell like? 10

Read chapter 10.
Read the Scriptures on p. 175 for chapter 10.

Discussion

1. Read John 12:44-49.

   a. Describe what you learned about the relationship between the Father and Jesus in this passage.

   b. What do you learn about judging and judgment in this passage? What does this mean to the believer and to the unbeliever?

2. Read II Peter 2:4-9.

    a. What happened to the ungodly angels?

    b. Compare the ungodly and godly people in this passage.

    c. Why do you think the Lord included this passage in the Bible?

3. Read Luke 16:19-31.

    a. Rich man:

        i. Describe the rich man's life while he was alive.

        ii. Describe how he is spending eternity.

b. Beggar:

   i. Describe the beggar's life while he was alive.

   ii. Describe how he is spending eternity. ("Abraham's side" figuratively defines a place of blessedness.)

   iii. Verse 26 talks about a "chasm." How do you picture this "chasm?"

Application

   iv. Finish. I desire to spend eternity with the rich man/beggar [circle one] because...

4. Read how Revelation 20:10 describes the "lake of burning sulfur."

   a. What image of the lake do you envision?

   b. Picture yourself in the "lake of burning sulfur" for eternity. What emotions arise in you?

   c. Is this how you want to spend eternity? (If you are not a believer in Jesus please read chapter 18 on page 161 to avoid this terrible fate of eternity in Hell!)

   d. If you're a Christian, imagine your acquaintances there. Do you want them to spend eternity there? Yes/No [circle one]. If you answered "No," write below how you plan to witness to them.

What is heaven like?

Read chapter 11.
Read the Scriptures on p. 176 for chapter 11.

Discussion

1. From the last four passages for chapter 11 on page 176, describe what you think Heaven will be like.

2. Read Revelation 21:1-5 and Revelation 22:1-5.

   a. Describe the New Jerusalem.

   b. Would you want to spend eternity in the New Jerusalem? Yes/No [circle one]. Why did you answer the way you did?

3. Read John 14:2-3.

   a. What is Jesus doing now?

   b. What are the two promises He gives us in verse 3?

Application

   c. If you do not know Christ as your personal Savior read chapter 18 on page 161.

   d. Finish the following statement based on John 14:2-3. Dear Jesus, I look forward to Your coming because...

4. In the previous chapter we got a glimpse of hell. In question 2 of this chapter we discussed the New Jerusalem. Each one of us will spend our eternity in either the New Jerusalem or Hell. Finish the following statement. I desire to spend eternity in heaven (New Jerusalem)/hell [circle one] because...[finish]

Note: If you want to spend eternity in the New Jerusalem (heaven) with our dear Lord, you must ask for His forgiveness of you sins. See chapter 18 on page 161.

When are you coming back?

Read chapter 12.
Read the Scriptures on p. 176 for chapter 12.

Discussion

1. Read Mark 13:32-37 and I Thessalonians 4:13-5:11. Mark 13 is a parable talking of our Savior as master. Answer these questions based on these Scriptures.

   a. How is Jesus' return described?

   b. When will Jesus come for us?

   c. For whom is Jesus coming in these passages?

d.　What do these passages say about the dead in Christ (i.e. Christians who have died)?

2.　Read Matthew 24:4-14.

　　　a.　Which of these signs do you see in the world now?

　　　b.　Which of these signs don't you see?

Application

3.　Finish this statement. I want to be ready for Jesus' return. I'll do this by (give a date and an action)...

4. Do you think Jesus is coming soon?

   a. Why or why not?

   b. How does your answer affect how you live?

Why is prayer important?

Read chapter 13.
Read the Scriptures on p. 177 for chapter 13.

Discussion

1. Read Psalm 119:97-104.

    a. What are some of the things the Psalmist meditates on?

    b. What are some benefits of meditation?

2. Read Philippians 4:8-9.

    a. What guidelines for thinking and meditating does Paul give?

b. How can Paul's guidelines be implemented in our daily lives?

Application

c. Finish the following meditation. Lord, You are so wonderful…

3. Prayers.

   a. Write a prayer to whisper to God before you get out of bed each day.

   b. Write a prayer to praise God for how caring and loving He has been to you.

c. Write a prayer to let God know how much you love Him.

4. Meditating.
    a. Write an outline to get started on meditating on the overwhelming idea that even before you were conceived God knew you and had exciting plans for you.

    b. Meditate using your outline as the starting point.

Why is worship important?

Read chapter 14.
Read the Scriptures on p. 178 for chapter 14.

Discussion

1. Praise – read Psalm 33.

    a. List the praise verses in Psalm 33.

    b. What does the Psalmist praise the Lord for?

    c. Write a praise in your own words to praise Him for these things.

d. What do you learn about the Lord in this chapter?

2. Read Psalm 100.

   a. Write verses 1 and 2 using your own words.

   b. Rewrite verse 3 in your own words.

   c. Verse 4 tells that as we enter places of worship we are to _____. The end of verse 4 tells us that we are to always:

d. Write a joyful paragraph thanking Him and praising Him. Then each night for one week before you fall asleep say or sing these words to our precious Lord.

e. Commit verse 5 to memory.

3. Copy I Chronicles 29:11-13 from your favorite version of the Bible and place it where you'll see it many times each day or carry it with you. At least 3 times each day for a week read this passage and worship the Lord.

Application

4. Read Exodus 20:1-6.

   a. Rewrite these verses in your own words.

b. Verse 3 is a clear, direct statement. Finish this sentence. I am not to...

c. Verses 5 and 6 contrast how the Lord deals with those who worship Him compared to those who do not. Fill in the following table.

Those who worship only God	Those who worship even one idol

d. Put verse 5 in your own words.

You want me to smell good?

Read chapter 15.
Read the Scriptures on p. 178 for chapter 15.

Discussion

1. Our fragrances.

    a. List three actions a Christian does that do not smell good to the Lord and tell why this is so.

        i.

        ii.

        iii.

b. List three actions a Christian does that are sweet fragrances to the Lord and tell why they are so delightful to the Lord.

   i.

   ii.

   iii.

2. Read Philippians 2:6–8.

   a. What do you learn about Jesus' obedience?

   b. What do you learn about the depth of Christ's love?

   c. What do you learn about the cost Christ paid for us?

3. Read Ephesians 5:1-2.

   a. Why do you obey the Lord?

   b. What does this mean for each believer?

4. We are to use Scriptures to counter Satan's temptation to sin. First define each of the following sins, then give at least one Scripture to counter the following sins. (Use a concordance.)

   a. Gossip.

      i. Definition:

      ii. Scripture(s):

   b. Lust.

      i. Definition:

      ii. Scripture(s):

   c. Envy.

      i. Definition:

      ii. Scripture(s):

Application

    d. What temptation(s) do you face? What verse(s) can help you avoid this (these) temptations(s)?

        i. Temptation(s):

        ii. Scripture(s):

5. Read I Corinthians 10:13 in several versions of the Bible.

    a. Rewrite this verse in your own words.

    b. Finish this statement. This verse means so much to me because...

    c. Memorize this verse to quote when you are tempted. (Psalm 119:11 gives the reason for memorizing verses.)

6. Many Scriptures for this chapter talk about loving others. Finish these statements.

    a. I really don't like (list specific individuals or groups, you may disguise names if others might see this page)...

    b. Write a prayer to love each of the above.

7. Now write a prayer of thanksgiving for those you dearly love.

You want me to wear the Emperor's clothes?

Read chapter 16.
Read the Scriptures on p. 179 for chapter 16.

Discussion

1. Read Matthew 24:4-14.

   a. Finish the following table.

Phrase	Definition
"...but the end is still to come..." (verse 6)	
"...the beginning of birth pangs" (verse 8)	
"...the end will come" (verse 14)	

b. Finish the following table.

Phrase	Answer
Events described in Matthew 24:1-14	
What's happening in the world today that fulfills these events partially?	
What's happening in the world today that fulfills these events completely?	

2. Read Ephesians 6:11-18.

   a. In your own words write the purpose of the following:

      i. Belt

      ii. Breastplate

      iii. Shoes

      iv. Shield of faith

      v. Helmet

      vi. Sword

Application

   b. Why put on God's armor (verse 11 and 13)?

   c. Rewrite verse 18 in your own words.

3. Read John 16:33.

   a. What promise does Jesus give each believer in this verse?

b. Write a prayer thanking God for the hope we have in this promise.

17

Your Majesty!

Read chapter 17.
Read the Scriptures on p. 180 for chapter 17.

Discussion/Application

1. Praise! Write 3 names followed by a prayer of praise e.g. *Savior* – Thank you, Jesus, for dying for me. You are so wonderful to suffer so harshly for me. What love to take my sins on Yourself. I love You so. What a wonderful Lord You are!

    a. Name:

       Prayer:

    b. Name:

       Prayer:

c. Name:

Prayer:

2. Teach me, Lord

   a. Select a name that defines a quality of the Lord that you want to know better.

   b. Study the Scriptures to learn more about this name. You may also want to use other resources such as *Strongs Concordance* or books from your church library.

      i. Write what you learn about this name here:

      ii. Write a prayer addressing the Lord by this name.

3. Select a name of the Lord that helps in each of the following situations and tell why.

   a. Difficult assignments at work/school/home.

b. Conflict with mate/best friend/parent.

c. Ethical issues.

d. Success:

　　i. In your vocation.

　　ii. In your avocation.

www.ingramcontent.com/pod-product-compliance
Lightning Source LLC
LaVergne TN
LVHW041457070426
835507LV00009B/652